,k You!

nt to extend my heartfelt thanks to you for choosing to bring "My First Day of
ergarten" into your home. As a writer, there is no greater joy than knowing that my
s have found their way into the hands of precious young readers like you.

e that this book will serve as a comforting and exciting companion as your little one
arks on this new chapter of their life. May it spark curiosity, ease nerves, and inspire a
for learning that will blossom with each turn of the page.

support and enthusiasm for this story mean everything to me, and I am humbled to be
rt of your child's literary journey. Thank you for welcoming "My First Day of
ergarten" into your family's collection of memories.

warmest regards,
Herbinko

Dear Jade,

As you embark on this exciting new adventure of starting kindergarten, I want to take a
moment to tell you how incredibly proud I am of you. This is such a big step, and I know
are going to shine bright like the little star that you are.

Kindergarten is a place where you will learn so many new things, make new friends, and
have lots of fun. Remember to be kind, curious, and brave. Your teachers are there to h
you grow and learn, and I know you will do amazing things in their care.

Always remember that no matter what happens, I am here for you, cheering you on eve
step of the way. You are such a smart, wonderful, and special little girl, and I can't wait t
see all the incredible things you will do in kindergarten and beyond.

Have a fantastic first day, my sweet Jade. Remember, you are loved more than you cou
ever imagine.

Love always,
Dad

Jade woke up early, feeling excited. Today was her first day of kindergarten! She had been waiting for this day for so long. She quickly got dressed and ran to the kitchen for breakfast.

Jade's mom made her favorite pancakes. They were shaped like stars and hearts. Jade giggled as she ate them. She felt special and ready for her big day.

After breakfast, Jade packed her new backpack. She put in her crayons, a notebook, and her favorite book. She also added a snack and a water bottle. Her mom helped her zip it up.

Jade and her mom walked to school hand in hand. The sun was shining, and the birds were singing. Jade felt a little nervous but mostly excited. She couldn't wait to see her new classroom.

When they arrived, Mrs. Brown, the kindergarten teacher, greeted them. She had a warm smile and kind eyes. Jade liked her immediately. Mrs. Brown showed Jade where to hang her backpack.

In the classroom, Jade saw many children her age. Some were playing with blocks, while others were drawing. Jade felt a bit shy at first. But soon, a girl named Emma came over and said hello.

Mrs. Brown rang a bell, and everyone gathered in a circle. She asked each child to say their name and favorite color. Jade said, 'My name is Jade, and my favorite color is Yellow.Everyone clapped for her.

Next, it was time for arts and crafts. Mrs. Brown gave everyone paper, glue, and glitter. Jade made a beautiful picture of a rainbow. She was proud of her work and showed it to Emma.

After arts and crafts, it was story time. Mrs. Brown read a story about a brave little mouse. Jade listened carefully, imagining herself as the mouse. She loved how the mouse solved problems.

Then, it was time for recess. Jade and Emma played on the swings and the slide. They laughed and had so much fun. Jade felt happy to have a new friend.

After recess, everyone went back inside for a snack. Jade took out her apple and juice box. She shared some crackers with Emma. They talked about their favorite games.

Mrs. Brown then taught the class about numbers. Jade learned to count to ten. She enjoyed the fun counting songs. Numbers were like a new adventure for her.

Later, the children played with building blocks. Jade and Emma built a tall tower together. They were careful not to let it fall. It was the tallest tower in the class!

Mrs. Brown played some music, and everyone danced. Jade loved the happy tunes and twirled around. Dancing made her feel free and joyful. She couldn't stop smiling.

The school day was almost over. Mrs. Brown gathered everyone for a goodbye song. Jade sang along with her new friends. She felt a little sad to leave but excited to come back.

Jade's mom came to pick her up. Jade told her all about her wonderful day. She couldn't wait to go back to kindergarten tomorrow. Jade knew she was going to love school.